ISLAMIC VALL
FOR CHILDREN

Lila Assiff-Tarabain

GOODWORD

Thoughtfulness and Exploration

Everything is created for a purpose. In the Qur'an, God tells us to explore creation and think what purpose each thing may have. The fascinating creatures on the earth and in the oceans; the sky and everything it carries; the magnificent mountains and the vastness of the Earth. Things may seem simple, until we explore them in detail. Then we cannot deny the miracle of creation. For example, as solid as the mountains are, we know that they store water and they moderate climate. Without exploring creation and thinking, we would never realize the miracles they hide. The Quran insists on our thinking all the time.

Appreciating Beauty

Believers are taught to love all of God's creation. A Muslim believes that everything created by God is complete and beautiful. Whenever we see something beautiful, whether in nature, or another person, we remember God, the Creator, saying "Glory be to God" (SubhanAllah). Beauty is not just what is on the surface. Beauty lies within our hearts. God sees what is in our hearts, so believers strive to keep their hearts beautiful and pure.

Thankfulness

We are thankful to God for our health, wealth, happiness, and life. It is reported that the Prophet Muhammad ﷺ said to look at those who have less than you, not more than you, so that you will be grateful for what God has given you. Whoever does not thank people, does not thank God. And the best way to thank the doer of good is to say, "May Allah reward you," because all praise is to God.

Caring for others

Islam teaches love and care for all of God's creation. Abusing anything is equivalent to being ungrateful for what God has provided. Showing kindness to animals pleases God. Believers are also obliged to visit the sick, and be kind to the elderly. God has given us the Earth to sustain us. Respecting that, Islam teaches the careful keeping of all resources, and prohibits wasting them.

5

Generosity and Sharing

The Prophet Muhammad ﷺ said: "None of you truly believes until he loves for his brother what he loves for himself." Believers are encouraged to give generously of their wealth to charity. This is a religious duty and is one of the five pillars of Islam. Islam discourages selfishness and encourages sharing, no matter how much or how little. Sharing in Islam includes material items, as well as wealth and acquired knowledge.

6

Sensitivity to suffering

Every believer must spend a portion of his wealth in charity. Special consideration must be given to widows, orphans, and those who are least able to support themselves. Gifts of money should be made to organizations which help disperse funds worldwide to feed the hungry, and help those who are suffering as a result of natural disasters, disease or war.

Mercy and Forgiveness

We show mercy to others so that God may show mercy to us. The Prophet Muhammad ﷺ tells us to show mercy to whoever and whatever is on Earth, and God in heaven will show mercy to us. God tells us in the Qur'an to show forgiveness and urge others to do what is good. God forgives us when we sincerely turn to Him for forgiveness. So when anyone asks for forgiveness, believers are encouraged to accept the apology and forgive.

Fairness and Justice

In Islam, if you are asked to judge between two people, or be a party to business dealings, you must do it fairly. There are strict and fair rules that govern buying and selling. There are also strict rules when judging between two parties. A Muslim should never take sides. He should always be on the side of justice, even if it harms his near and dear ones.

Moreover, the Prophet Muhammad ﷺ advised that a judge should not make a decision between two persons when he was in an angry mood, because this would affect his reasoning. Stress is laid on the concepts of fairness and justice throughout the Qur'an. Those who bear false witness will be punished.

9

Living by the rules

Islamic life is governed by the Qur'an and the Sunnah (the life of the Prophet Muhammad ﷺ). We live by the rules when we perform the five daily prayers at their set time, and when we fast during the month of Ramadan. We live by the rules of our religion, so that we will live orderly lives. We live by the rules when we obey the laws of the country in which we live. A Muslim is always law-abiding.

Accountability to God

The Prophet Muhammad ﷺ once said that the best person is the one who is fair when selling, buying or making demands. We become upright citizens when we remember that we shall have to justify all that we say and do before God, and that every deed and intention is recorded. Eventually, we shall all be held accountable for every lie we tell and every fraud we commit, and shall be punished and rewarded accordingly.

Being Self-Disciplined and Serene

During the holy month of Ramadan, believers exercise self-discipline by not eating or drinking all day. Especially during this month, serenity is achieved when the fasting person knows that he/she is not doing anything wrong, not losing his/her temper, and is aware that it is for God that he/she is observing the month of fasting. By regularly reading the Qur'an, the believer achieves peace of mind and is reminded that God has given us life to worship Him alone, and that we should not become lost in worldly matters.

11

Modesty and Humility

Protecting one's modesty is a major rule in Islam. Both men and women are expected to show modesty in all aspects of their lives. Not only are believers expected to dress modestly, but we should be modest in the

ways we talk, walk, eat and generally behave in society. Islam does not excuse any kind of bragging or showing off, because arrogance is sinful. A Muslim is always humble. He can never be proud. We show respect to others by listening to what they have to say.

Cultivating Brotherhood

Islam rises above all barriers of colour and nationality by bringing to humanity a sense of brotherhood. It is not only that every Muslim is the brother of other Muslims: he is the brother of all men. Islam brings people fromall walks of life, from all over the world together. It knits the whole of mankind

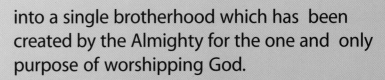

into a single brotherhood which has been created by the Almighty for the one and only purpose of worshipping God.

Unity and Harmony

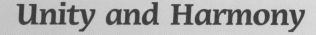

Fearing God and remaining aware of the bad results of wrongdoing create unity and harmony among mankind. The essence of unity and harmony is summed up in the Islamic greeting "Peace be unto you" and it is the believer's duty always to greet others with these words (*salam*).

The Prophet Muhammad ﷺ taught that living harmoniously meant helping one another, not looking for faults in one another, staying clear of envy, not being angry with one another and being good to neighbours, whatever their faith. Regardless of wealth and social position, Muslims pray side by side. This helps to strengthen unity among Muslims. This unity, which is marked by harmonious living, is extended by them to non-Muslims also. All people are created equal, and we are all servants of God.

14

Willingness to lead

It is the duty of each Muslim to take part in the weekly Friday prayer, which is said in groups, usually in mosques. This encourages all members of the community to meet each other regularly. Attending weddings, funerals, visiting the sick, and joining in the various religious celebrations all maintain the bonds of kinship and community. Social ties are also strengthened by hosting meals on occasions. Being a good Muslim means being a positive role model and a good leader within society and always doing something positive to further its growth. A Muslim is always ahead of others in doing good work.

Learning and Spreading Message of the Quran

The stories of the prophets and the civilizations before us have all been clearly recorded in the Qur'an. Studying the Qur'an reminds us that, as different as we all are today, we are all descendants of the Prophet Abraham ﷺ. We are all the children of the Prophet Adam ﷺ. The Qur'an tells us of important events that occurred in ancient times, so that we can learn from them, and have respect for the ordeals endured by the prophets in conveying God's message. It is the duty of a Muslim to share and spread the message of Quran, the word of God, to the rest of the world.

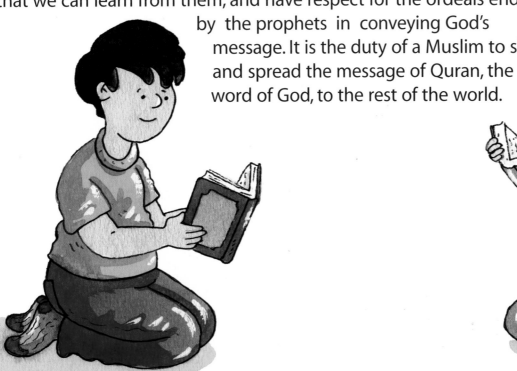

Faithfullness and Steadfastness

Muslims have complete faith in God. Their faith is based on reason and rationality. That is why it is so strong. We have a duty to pray to God at least five times a day. Taking care to say our daily prayers sustains our faith in God and brings us closer to God, since being regular in prayer is what makes us stronger in our faith.

FAJR

DHUHR

ASR

MAGHRIB

ISHA

Hope and Patience

A believer is always hopeful and patient, because his faith in God is absolute. Knowing that God is forgiving brings hope to those who sincerely repent to God and who never repeat their mistakes. Also, knowing that a fair judgement will be made in the afterlife brings peace to each individual who has suffered an injustice in this life. Whether a deed is good or not depends on the intention behind the deed. God knows everything. Nothing can be hidden from Him. There will be rewards for all good deeds and punishments for all misdeeds in the Final Judgement.

Courage!!!

Courageous and Confidence

Our trust in God is our safeguard from every kind of fear or danger. Our faith in God gives us courage and confidence to face anything. When we put our full trust in God, while having taken reasonable precautions, we don't have to fear anything. God causes everything to happen for a reason. And everything that happens is in our best interests, though we may not understand this right away.

19

Seeking of Knowledge

The first word sent down in the Qur'an was "Read!" God encourages mankind to strive for knowledge. All of our knowledge comes as a gift from God. When knowledge is received, it is the duty of the believer to share that knowledge with others. God has allowed mankind to be curious about things. By being curious, a person acquires knowledge or sees new meaning in the way we understand things. No knowledge is withheld from man if he is curious enough and tries hard to find it.

THERE IS NO GOD BUT ALLAH AND MUHAMMAD IS THE MESSENGER OF ALLAH

Honesty and Truthfullness

First and foremost, we must be honest and truthful to ourselves. By stating that "there is no god but Allah, and Muhammad is the messenger of Allah," we are saying out loud what is truly in our hearts. If a 'believer' does not truly believe this, he is nothing but a hypocrite. We must be open, honest and truthful when dealing with others. Speaking the truth leads to goodness and this virtue leads to paradise. A Muslim never lies.

21

Realism and Self Criticism

We are self-critical when we remember that all success is due to God's goodness and mercy and not to one's own strengths. Believers are realistic. We try to be humble before God and confess our weaknesses and seek God's grace. The Prophet ﷺ once said that, for those who realized their own limitations and weaknesses, there would be blessings. Knowing one's weaknesses helps a person be less critical of others.

Being a Lover of Peace

Islam is a religion of peace. The Quran calls its way the 'paths of peace'. God greatly dislikes those who are quarrelsome in nature. A Muslim at all costs avoids aggression and violence and strives to keep the peace. He firmly believes that making up with others is the best policy. A Muslim is surely a peace lover. Paradise is the abode of Peace.

Reflection and Spirituality

The signs of creation are all around us! We cannot deny holy creation when we look at the stars, the planets, the order of night and day, the passage of time, the mountains and the sky. God repeatedly tells us in the Qur'an to look at and ponder upon creation, and become aware of how the magnificence of the order of creation must come from a higher Being. This brings us closer to God, as we understand Him in His all splendour. We learn to live a life which obeys God's will and which is full of inner meanings and is not materialistic in nature. This is how one becomes a spiritual person. This is what the true worship of God is about.

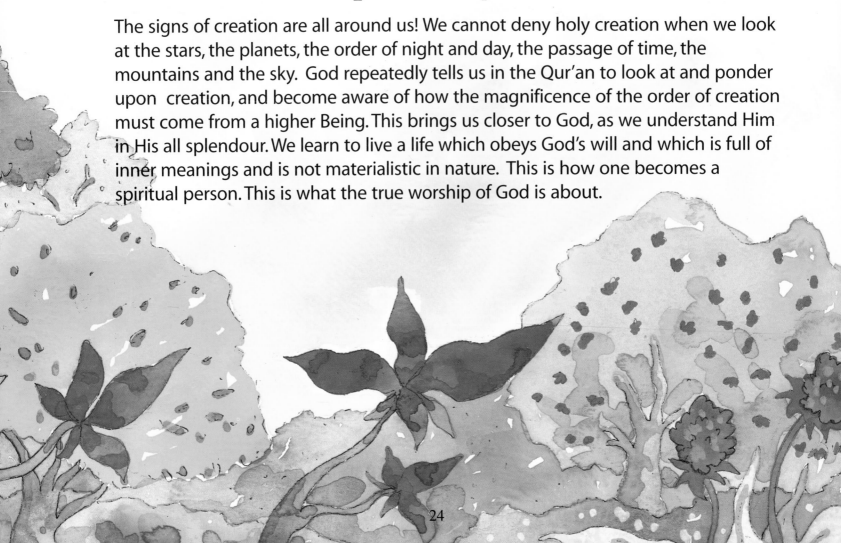